HAL•LEONARD

PIANO VOCAL GUITAR

ESSENTIAL SONGS

The 1930s

ISBN 0-634-09106-9

HAL•LEONARD®
CORPORATION

7777 W. BLUEMOUND RD. P.O. BOX 13819 MILWAUKEE, WI 53213

Visit Hal Leonard Online at
www.halleonard.com

CONTENTS

209	It's the Talk of the Town	Jerry Livingston/Marty Symes/Al Neiburg	1933
212	June in January	Leo Robin/Ralph Rainger	1934
220	Just a Gigolo	Leonello Casucci/Julius Brammer/Irving Caesar	1930
215	Just One More Chance	Arthur Johnston/Sam Coslow	1931
224	The Lady Is a Tramp	Richard Rodgers/Lorenz Hart	1937
228	The Lady's in Love with You	Burton Lane/Frank Loesser	1939
231	Lazy River	Hoagy Carmichael/Sidney Arodin	1931
234	Let's Face the Music and Dance	Irving Berlin	1935
238	Little Girl Blue	Richard Rodgers/Lorenz Hart	1935
244	Little White Lies	Walter Donaldson	1930
252	Love in Bloom	Leo Robin/Ralph Rainger	1934
256	Love Is Just Around the Corner	Leo Robin/Lewis E. Gensler	1934
247	Lover	Richard Rodgers/Lorenz Hart	1932
260	Mood Indigo	Duke Ellington/Albany Bigard/Irving Mills	1931
264	Moonglow	Will Hudson/Eddie De Lange/Irving Mills	1934
268	My Baby Just Cares for Me	Walter Donaldson/Gus Kahn	1930
272	My Funny Valentine	Richard Rodgers/Lorenz Hart	1937
282	My Heart Belongs to Daddy	Cole Porter	1938
286	My Old Flame	Arthur Johnston/Sam Coslow	1934
290	My Romance	Richard Rodgers/Lorenz Hart	1935
277	My Silent Love	Dana Suesse/Edward Heyman	1932
294	The Nearness of You	Hoagy Carmichael/Ned Washington	1937
304	On the Sunny Side of the Street	Jimmy McHugh/Dorothy Fields	1930
308	Out of Nowhere	Johnny Green/Edward Heyman	1931
312	Pennies from Heaven	Arthur Johnston/John Burke	1936
316	Poinciana (Song of the Tree)	Nat Simon/Buddy Bernier	1936
318	Puttin' On the Ritz	Irving Berlin	1930
299	Rockin' Chair	Hoagy Carmichael	1932
322	Say It Isn't So	Irving Berlin	1932
330	September Song	Kurt Weill/Maxwell Anderson	1938
325	Sing, You Sinners	Sam Coslow/W. Franke Harling	1930
334	Small Fry	Frank Loesser/Hoagy Carmichael	1938
338	Smoke Gets in Your Eyes	Jerome Kern/Otto Harbach	1933
341	Soft Lights and Sweet Music	Irving Berlin	1931
346	The Song Is You	Jerome Kern/Oscar Hammerstein II	1932
350	Stormy Weather (Keeps Rainin' All the Time)	Harold Arlen/Ted Koehler	1933
354	Ten Cents a Dance	Richard Rodgers/Lorenz Hart	1930
362	Thanks for the Memory	Leo Robin/Ralph Rainger	1937
366	There Is No Greater Love	Isham Jones/Marty Symes	1936
359	There's a Small Hotel	Richard Rodgers/Lorenz Hart	1936
370	This Can't Be Love	Richard Rodgers/Lorenz Hart	1938
378	Two Sleepy People	Hoagy Carmichael/Frank Loesser	1938
373	The Very Thought of You	Ray Noble	1934
382	The Way You Look Tonight	Jerome Kern/Dorothy Fields	1936
385	What's New?	Bob Haggart/Johnny Burke	1939
388	Where or When	Richard Rodgers/Lorenz Hart	1937
392	Yesterdays	Jerome Kern/Otto Harbach	1933
398	You Are My Sunshine	Jimmie Davis/Charles Mitchell	1930
394	You Brought a New Kind of Love to Me	Sammy Fain/Irving Kahal/Pierre Norman	1930

ALL THE THINGS YOU ARE

from VERY WARM FOR MAY

Lyrics by OSCAR HAMMERSTEIN II
Music by JEROME KERN

APRIL IN PARIS

Words by E.Y. HARBURG
Music by VERNON DUKE

AUTUMN IN NEW YORK

Words and Music by
VERNON DUKE

14

BEYOND THE BLUE HORIZON
from the Paramount Picture MONTE CARLO

Words by LEO ROBIN
Music by RICHARD A. WHITING
and W. FRANKE HARLING

BETWEEN THE DEVIL AND THE DEEP BLUE SEA

from RHYTHMANIA

Lyric by TED KOEHLER
Music by HAROLD ARLEN

BODY AND SOUL

Words by EDWARD HEYMAN,
ROBERT SOUR and FRANK EYTON
Music by JOHN GREEN

BOO-HOO

Lyric and Music by EDWARD HEYMAN,
CARMEN LOMBARDO and JOHN JACOB LOEB

CARAVAN
from SOPHISTICATED LADIES

Words and Music by DUKE ELLINGTON,
IRVING MILLS and JUAN TIZOL

CHANGE PARTNERS

from the RKO Radio Motion Picture CAREFREE

Words and Music by
IRVING BERLIN

Must you dance _____ ev - 'ry dance _____ with the same _____ for - tu - nate man? _____ You have

Ask him to sit this one out, and while you're a - lone

I'll tell the wait - er to tell him he's

want - ed on the tel - e - phone. You've been locked

in his arms

CHEEK TO CHEEK
from the RKO Radio Motion Picture TOP HAT

Words and Music by
IRVING BERLIN

48

CHEROKEE
(Indian Love Song)

Words and Music by
RAY NOBLE

COCKTAILS FOR TWO
from the Paramount Picture MURDER AT THE VANITIES

Words and Music by ARTHUR JOHNSTON
and SAM COSLOW

EAST OF THE SUN
(And West of the Moon)

Words and Music by
BROOKS BOWMAN

DON'T BLAME ME

Words by DOROTHY FIELDS
Music by JIMMY McHUGH

Ev - er since the luck - y night I found you ____ I've hung a - round you, ____ just like a
I like ev - 'ry sin - gle thing a - bout you ____ with - out a doubt you ____ are like a

fool fall - ing head and heels in love like a kid out of
dream. In my mind I find a pic - ture of us as a

EASTER PARADE

featured in the Motion Picture Irving Berlin's EASTER PARADE
from AS THOUSANDS CHEER

Words and Music by
IRVING BERLIN

EASY LIVING
Theme from the Paramount Picture EASY LIVING

Words and Music by LEO ROBIN
and RALPH RAINGER

EASY TO LOVE
(You'd Be So Easy to Love)
from BORN TO DANCE

Words and Music by
COLE PORTER

FALLING IN LOVE AGAIN
(Can't Help It)
from the Paramount Picture THE BLUE ANGEL

Words by SAMMY LERNER
Music by FREDERICK HOLLANDER

THE FOLKS WHO LIVE ON THE HILL

from HIGH, WIDE AND HANDSOME

Lyrics by OSCAR HAMMERSTEIN II
Music by JEROME KERN

FALLING IN LOVE WITH LOVE
from THE BOYS FROM SYRACUSE

Words by LORENZ HART
Music by RICHARD RODGERS

A FINE ROMANCE

from SWING TIME

Words by DOROTHY FIELDS
Music by JEROME KERN

Moderately

She: A fine ro - mance! With no good
kiss - es! A fine ro - mance, my
fel - low! You take ro - mance, I'll

friend, this is! We should be like a
take jel - lo! You're calm - er than the

FOR ALL WE KNOW

Words by SAM M. LEWIS
Music by J. FRED COOTS

Moderately slow

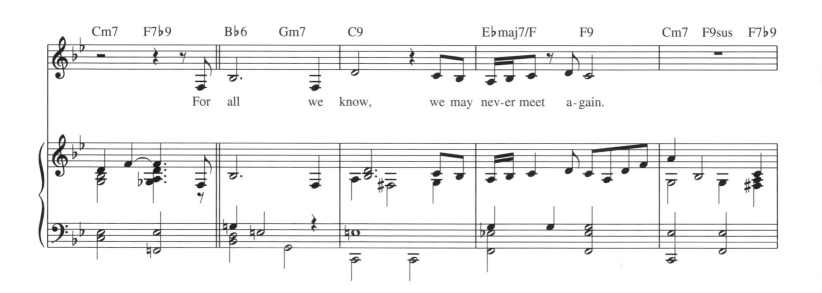

For all we know, we may nev-er meet a-gain.

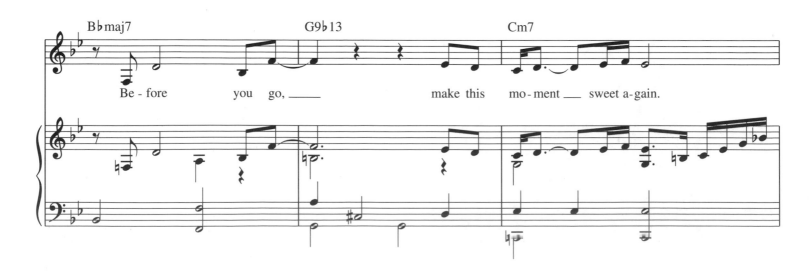

Be - fore you go, ___ make this mo-ment ___ sweet a-gain.

GEORGIA ON MY MIND

Words by STUART GORRELL
Music by HOAGY CARMICHAEL

THE GLORY OF LOVE
from GUESS WHO'S COMING TO DINNER

Words and Music by
BILLY HILL

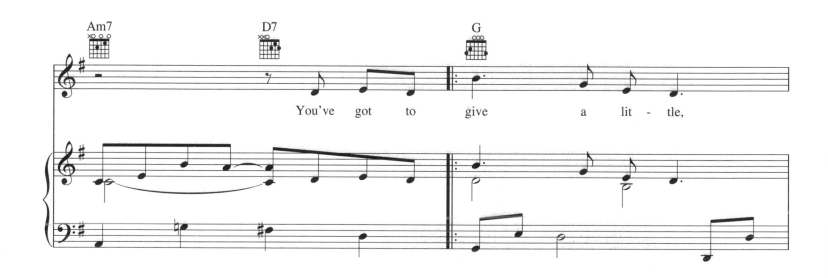

You've got to give a lit-tle,

take a lit-tle, and let your poor heart break a lit-tle.

HARBOR LIGHTS

Words and Music by
JIMMY KENNEDY and HUGH WILLIAMS

Slowly (with expression)

HEART AND SOUL

from the Paramount Short Subject A SONG IS BORN

Words by FRANK LOESSER
Music by HOAGY CARMICHAEL

HEARTACHES

Words by JOHN KLENNER
Music by AL HOFFMAN

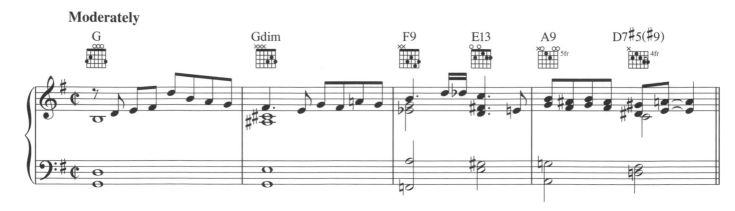

You said you loved me just as I love you, _____

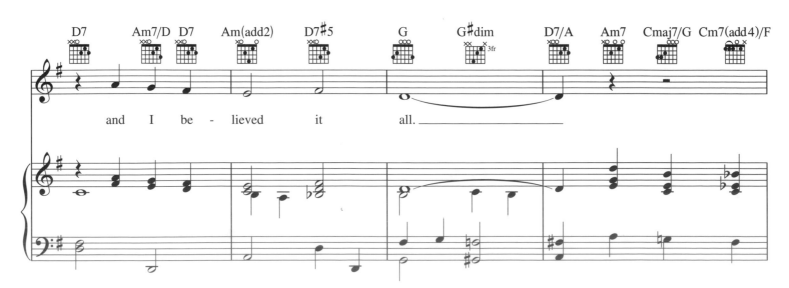

and I be - lieved it all. _____

118

HONEYSUCKLE ROSE

from AIN'T MISBEHAVIN'
from TIN PAN ALLEY

Words by ANDY RAZAF
Music by THOMAS "FATS" WALLER

HOW DEEP IS THE OCEAN
(How High Is the Sky)

Words and Music by
IRVING BERLIN

Lyrics:
How much do I love you? I'll tell you no lie, how deep is the o-cean, how high is the sky? How man-y

125

I CAN'T GET STARTED WITH YOU

from ZIEGFELD FOLLIES

Words by IRA GERSHWIN
Music by VERNON DUKE

I DON'T STAND A GHOST OF A CHANCE

Words by BING CROSBY and NED WASHINGTON
Music by VICTOR YOUNG

I FOUND A MILLION DOLLAR BABY
(In a Five and Ten Cent Store)
from FUNNY LADY

Lyric by BILLY ROSE and MORT DIXON
Music by HARRY WARREN

Love comes a-long like a pop-u-lar song, an-y-time or an-y-where at
Love used to be quite a strang-er to me, did-n't know a sen-ti-men-tal

all. Rain or sun-shine, spring or
word. Thoughts of kiss-ing seemed ab-

fall, you nev-er know when it may say hel-lo in a
surd. Then came a change, and you may think it strange, but the

I LIKE THE LIKES OF YOU

Words by E.Y. HARBURG
Music by VERNON DUKE

Allegretto

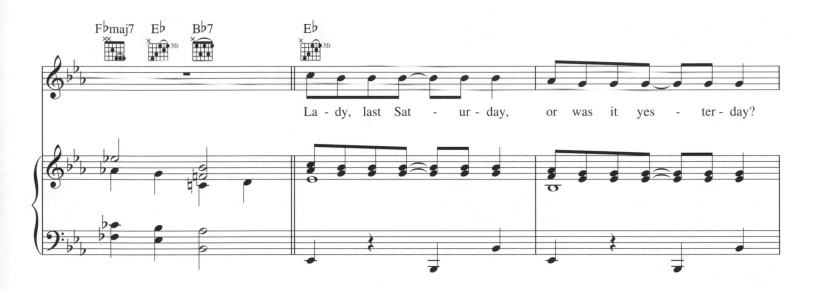

La - dy, last Sat - ur - day, or was it yes - ter - day?

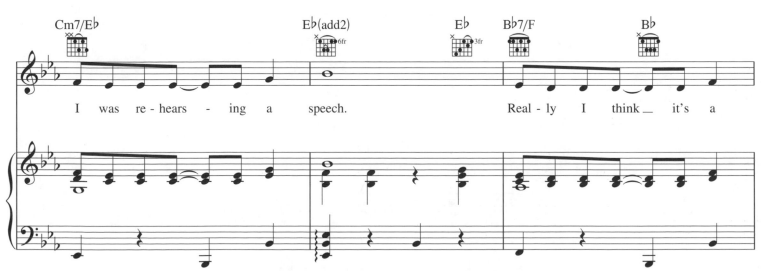

I was re-hears - ing a speech.   Real - ly I think ___ it's a

I like the likes of you, I like the things you

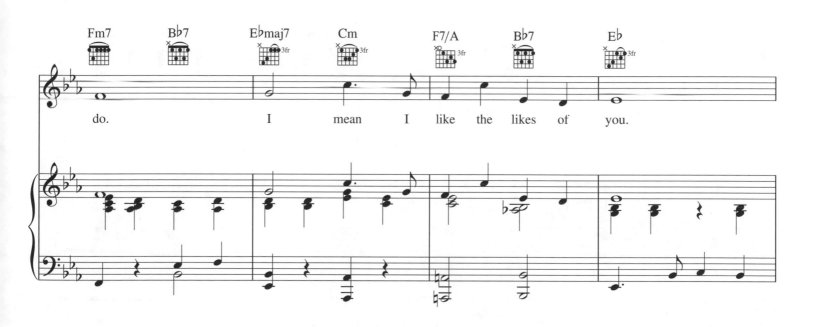

do. I mean I like the likes of you.

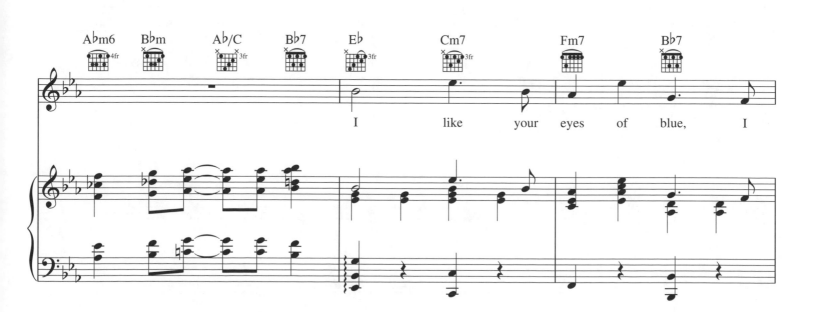

I like your eyes of blue, I

I like the likes of you. Your looks are pure de-

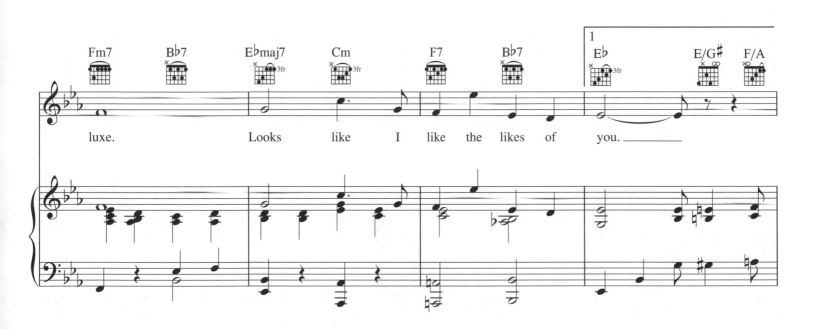

luxe. Looks like I like the likes of you. _____

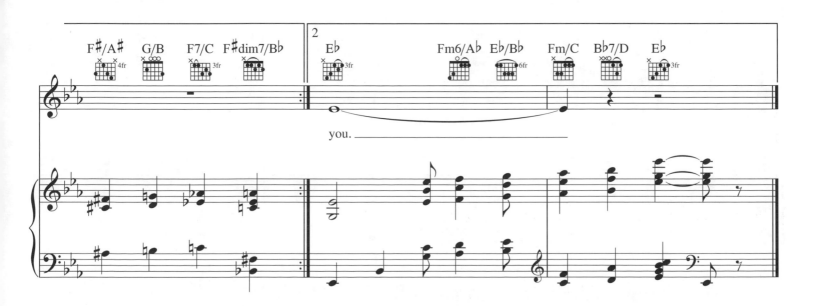

you. _____

I LET A SONG GO OUT OF MY HEART

Words and Music by DUKE ELLINGTON,
HENRY NEMO, JOHN REDMOND and IRVING MILLS

I WON'T DANCE

from ROBERTA

Words and Music by JIMMY McHUGH, DOROTHY FIELDS,
JEROME KERN, OSCAR HAMMERSTEIN II
and OTTO HARBACH

bumped on the shore. _____ I feel so ab-so-lute-ly

stumped on the floor! _____

She: When you dance you're charm-ing and you're gen - tle! _____

'Spec-'lly when you do the "Con - ti -

I'LL BE SEEING YOU

from RIGHT THIS WAY

Lyric by IRVING KAHAL
Music by SAMMY FAIN

Ca-the-dral bells were toll-ing _____ And our hearts sang on, _____

_ Was it the spell of Par-is _____ Or the A-pril dawn? _____

I'LL NEVER SMILE AGAIN

Words and Music by
RUTH LOWE

I'VE GOT THE WORLD ON A STRING

Lyric by TED KOEHLER
Music by HAROLD ARLEN

I'M PUTTING ALL MY EGGS IN ONE BASKET

from the Motion Picture FOLLOW THE FLEET

Words and Music by
IRVING BERLIN

I've been a roam-ing Ju-li-et, my Ro-me-os __ have been man-y,

but now my roam-ing days __ have __ gone. __

Too man-y i-rons in the fire __ is worse than not hav-ing an-y.

172

I'VE GOT MY LOVE TO KEEP ME WARM

from the 20th Century Fox Motion Picture ON THE AVENUE

Words and Music by
IRVING BERLIN

Bright jump tempo

I'VE GOT YOU UNDER MY SKIN

from BORN TO DANCE

Words and Music by
COLE PORTER

IN A SENTIMENTAL MOOD

Words and Music by DUKE ELLINGTON,
IRVING MILLS and MANNY KURTZ

IN THE MOOD

By JOE GARLAND

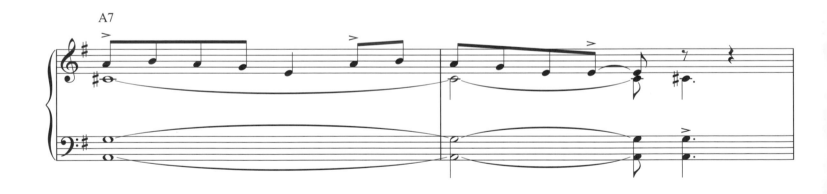

IN THE STILL OF THE NIGHT
from ROSALIE

Words and Music by
COLE PORTER

Moderately, mysteriously

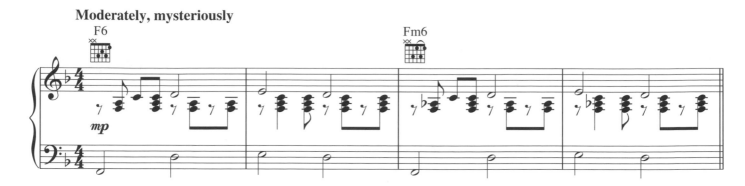

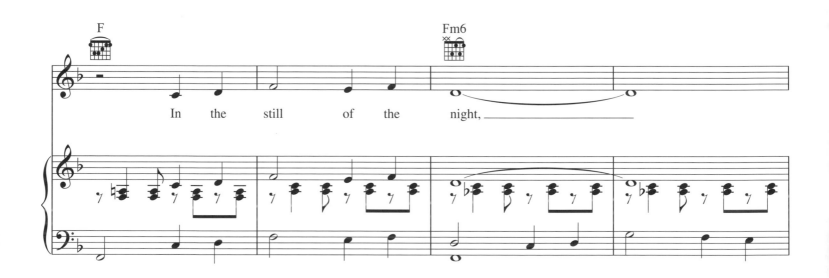

In the still of the night,

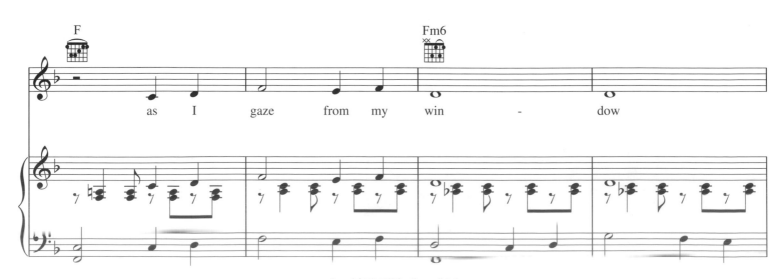

as I gaze from my win - dow

ISN'T IT ROMANTIC?

from the Paramount Picture LOVE ME TONIGHT

Words by LORENZ HART
Music by RICHARD RODGERS

IT'S DE-LOVELY
from RED, HOT AND BLUE!

Words and Music by
COLE PORTER

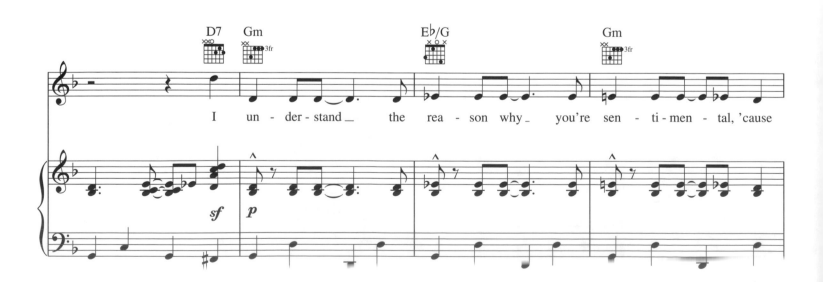

*Pronounced "delukes"

IT'S EASY TO REMEMBER

from the Paramount Picture MISSISSIPPI

Words by LORENZ HART
Music by RICHARD RODGERS

IT'S ONLY A PAPER MOON

from the Musical Production THE GREAT MAGOO

Lyric by BILLY ROSE and E.Y. HARBURG
Music by HAROLD ARLEN

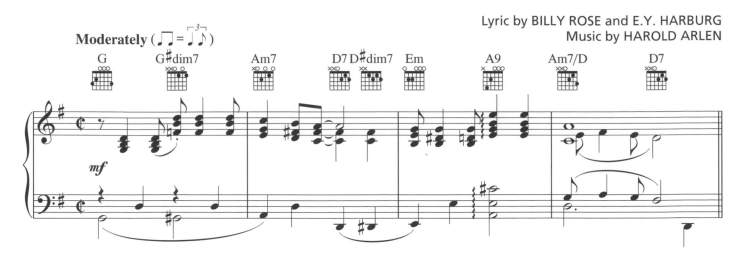

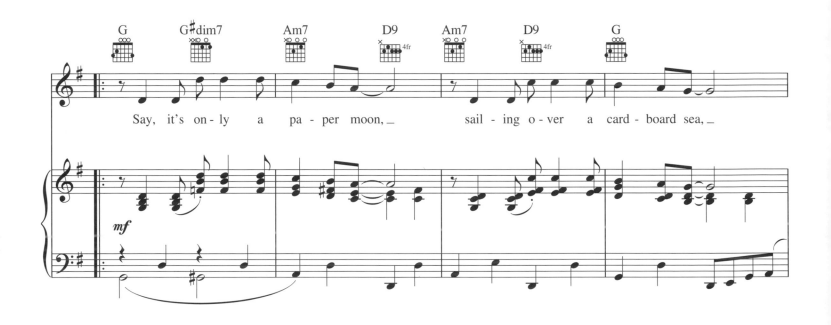

Say, it's on-ly a pa-per moon, __ sail-ing o-ver a card-board sea, __

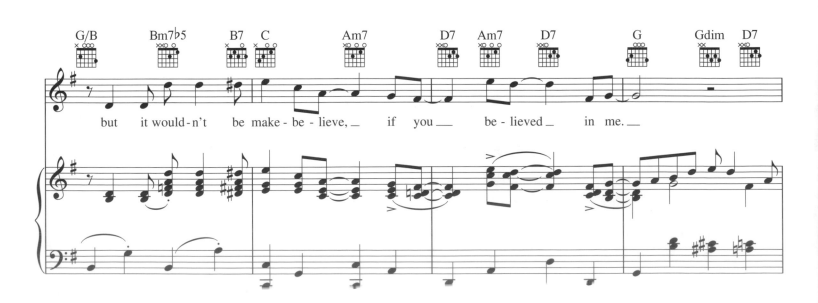

but it would-n't be make-be-lieve, __ if you __ be-lieved __ in me. __

IT'S THE TALK OF THE TOWN

Words by MARTY SYMES and AL NEIBURG
Music by JERRY LIVINGSTON

Slowly, with expression

JUNE IN JANUARY
from the Paramount Picture HERE IS MY HEART

Words and Music by LEO ROBIN
and RALPH RAINGER

JUST ONE MORE CHANCE

Words by SAM COSLOW
Music by ARTHUR JOHNSTON

JUST A GIGOLO

Original German Text by JULIUS BRAMMER
English Words by IRVING CAESAR
Music by LEONELLO CASUCCI

222

THE LADY IS A TRAMP

from BABES IN ARMS
from WORDS AND MUSIC

Words by LORENZ HART
Music by RICHARD RODGERS

THE LADY'S IN LOVE WITH YOU
from the Paramount Picture SOME LIKE IT HOT

Words by FRANK LOESSER
Music by BURTON LANE

Refrain

Long be-fore the first kiss___ have you ev-er seen this?___

If there's a gleam in her eye___ each time she straight-ens your tie,___ you'll know the la-dy's in love___ with you. If she can dress for a date___ with-out that wait-ing you hate___ it means the la-dy's in love___

230

LAZY RIVER

from THE BEST YEARS OF OUR LIVES

Words and Music by HOAGY CARMICHAEL
and SIDNEY ARODIN

LET'S FACE THE MUSIC AND DANCE

from the Motion Picture FOLLOW THE FLEET

Words and Music by
IRVING BERLIN

LITTLE GIRL BLUE
from JUMBO

Words by LORENZ HART
Music by RICHARD RODGERS

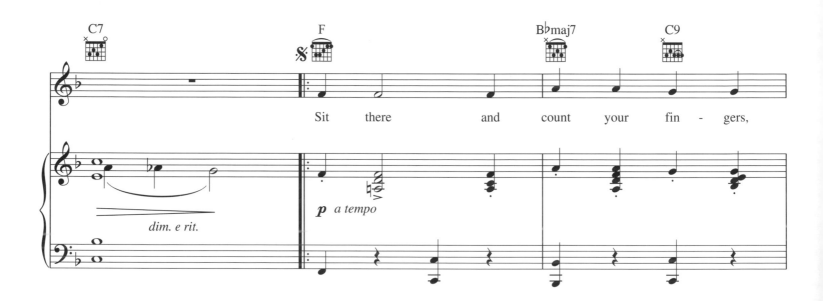

Sit there and count your fin - gers,

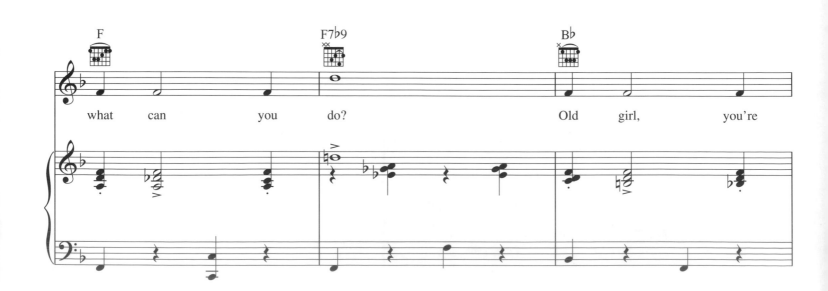

what can you do? Old girl, you're

won't some-bod-y send a ten - der

Blue boy to cheer a lit-tle girl blue?

blue?

When I was ver-y young _____ the world was

LITTLE WHITE LIES

Words and Music by
WALTER DONALDSON

* Symbols for Guitar and Tenor Banjo

LOVER
from the Paramount Picture LOVE ME TONIGHT

Words by LORENZ HART
Music by RICHARD RODGERS

LOVE IN BLOOM

from the Paramount Picture SHE LOVES ME NOT
from THE JACK BENNY SHOW

Words and Music by LEO ROBIN
and RALPH RAINGER

LOVE IS JUST AROUND THE CORNER

from the Paramount Picture HERE IS MY HEART

Words and Music by LEO ROBIN
and LEWIS E. GENSLER

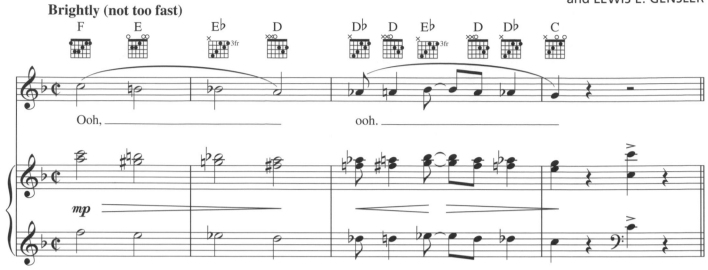

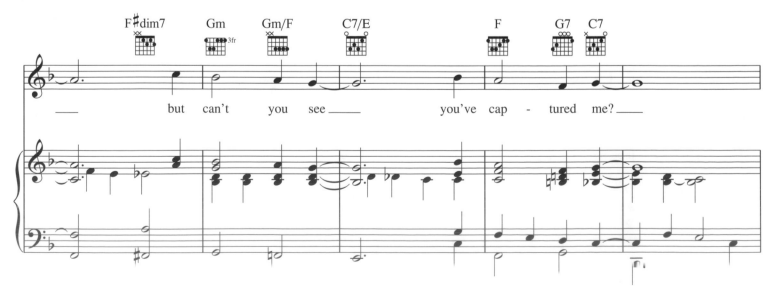

MOOD INDIGO

from SOPHISTICATED LADIES

Words and Music by DUKE ELLINGTON,
IRVING MILLS and ALBANY BIGARD

MOONGLOW

Words and Music by WILL HUDSON,
EDDIE DE LANGE and IRVING MILLS

MY BABY JUST CARES FOR ME

from WHOOPEE!

Lyrics by GUS KAHN
Music by WALTER DONALDSON

some-one loves me too. Guess it's hard for you to see just what an-y-one can see in me but it sim-ply goes to prove what love can do.

My ba-by don't care for shows, My ba-by don't
My ba-by's no Gil-bert fan, Ron Col-man is

MY FUNNY VALENTINE
from BABES IN ARMS

Words by LORENZ HART
Music by RICHARD RODGERS

MY SILENT LOVE

Words by EDWARD HEYMAN
Music by DANA SUESSE

MY HEART BELONGS TO DADDY

from LEAVE IT TO ME

Words and Music by
COLE PORTER

284

MY OLD FLAME
from the Paramount Picture BELLE OF THE NINETIES

Words and Music by ARTHUR JOHNSTON
and SAM COSLOW

The mu-sic seemed to be so rem-i-nis-cent; ___ I

knew I'd heard it some-where be-fore. I racked my rec-ol-lec-tions as I

lis-tened, ___ when sud-den-ly I ___ re-mem-bered once more. ___

288

MY ROMANCE
from JUMBO

Words by LORENZ HART
Music by RICHARD RODGERS

THE NEARNESS OF YOU
from the Paramount Picture ROMANCE IN THE DARK

Words by NED WASHINGTON
Music by HOAGY CARMICHAEL

ROCKIN' CHAIR

Words and Music by
HOAGY CARMICHAEL

ON THE SUNNY SIDE OF THE STREET

Lyric by DOROTHY FIELDS
Music by JIMMY McHUGH

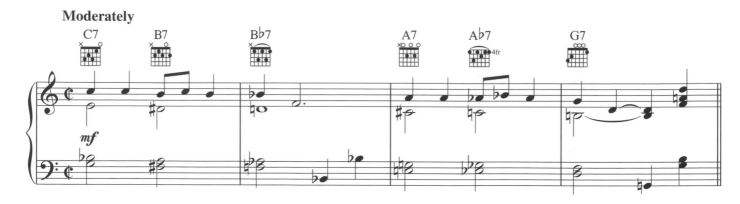

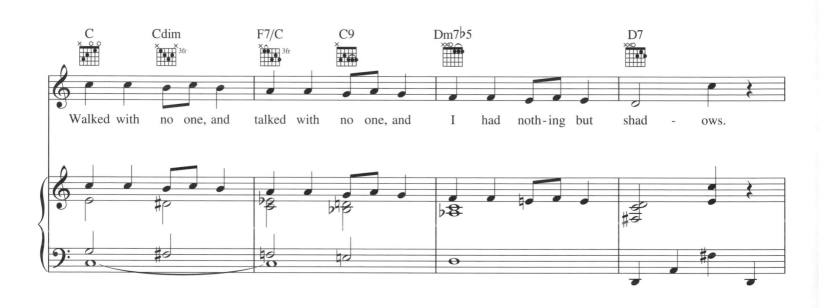

Walked with no one, and talked with no one, and I had noth-ing but shad - ows.

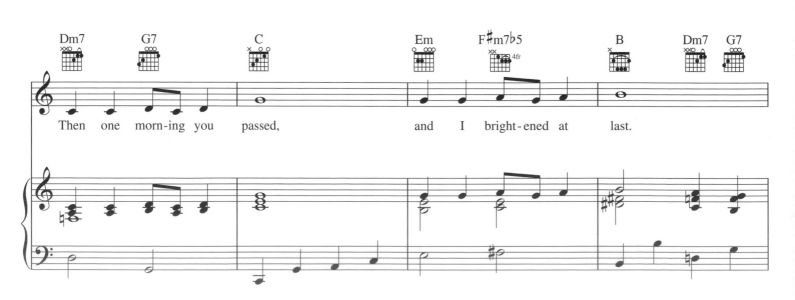

Then one morn-ing you passed, and I bright-ened at last.

OUT OF NOWHERE
from the Paramount Picture DUDE RANCH

Words by EDWARD HEYMAN
Music by JOHNNY GREEN

PENNIES FROM HEAVEN

from PENNIES FROM HEAVEN

Words by JOHN BURKE
Music by ARTHUR JOHNSTON

POINCIANA
(Song of the Tree)

Words by BUDDY BERNIER
Music by NAT SIMON

PUTTIN' ON THE RITZ
from the Motion Picture PUTTIN' ON THE RITZ

Words and Music by
IRVING BERLIN

SAY IT ISN'T SO

Words and Music by
IRVING BERLIN

SING, YOU SINNERS

(From The Paramount Picture "HONEY")
Theme from the Paramount Picture SING, YOU SINNERS

Words and Music by SAM COSLOW
and W. FRANKE HARLING

SEPTEMBER SONG
from the Musical Play KNICKERBOCKER HOLIDAY

Words by MAXWELL ANDERSON
Music by KURT WEILL

SMALL FRY

from the Paramount Picture SING, YOU SINNERS

Words by FRANK LOESSER
Music by HOAGY CARMICHAEL

Here comes that good-for-noth-in' brat of a boy; __ he's such a dev-il I could whip him with joy. __ He's been ca-rous-in' at the bur-ley-cue. __

SMOKE GETS IN YOUR EYES

from ROBERTA

Words by OTTO HARBACH
Music by JEROME KERN

SOFT LIGHTS AND SWEET MUSIC

from the Stage Production FACE THE MUSIC

Words and Music by
IRVING BERLIN

I can't re - sist the moan of a cel - lo, _____

THE SONG IS YOU
from MUSIC IN THE AIR

Lyrics by OSCAR HAMMERSTEIN II
Music by JEROME KERN

I hear mu-sic when I look at you, _____ a beau-ti-ful theme of ev-'ry dream I ev-er knew. _____ Down deep in my heart, _____ I hear it play. _____ I feel it

STORMY WEATHER
(Keeps Rainin' All the Time)
from COTTON CLUB PARADE OF 1933
featured in the Motion Picture STORMY WEATHER

Lyric by TED KOEHLER
Music by HAROLD ARLEN

Don't know why there's no sun up in the sky, Storm-y Weath-er,

Since my man and I ain't to-geth-er, keeps rain-in' all the time.

Life is bare, gloom and mis-'ry ev-'ry-where, Storm-y Weath-er,

Interlude

I walk a-round, heav-y heart-ed and sad. __ Night comes a-round and I'm

still feel-in' bad. __ Rain __ pour-in' down, blind-in' ev-'ry hope I had. This

pit-ter-in' pat-ter-in' beat-in' an' splat-ter-in' drives __ me mad, Love, love,

love, love, __ this mis-er-y is just too much for me. _____ Can't go

TEN CENTS A DANCE

from SIMPLE SIMON

Words by LORENZ HART
Music by RICHARD RODGERS

I work at the Pal - ace Ball - room, but, gee, that pal - ace is

cheap. When I get back to my chill - y hall room I'm much too ti - red to

sleep. I'm one of those la - dy teach - ers, a beau - ti - ful host - ess, you

355

THERE'S A SMALL HOTEL
from ON YOUR TOES

Words by LORENZ HART
Music by RICHARD RODGERS

THANKS FOR THE MEMORY

from the Paramount Picture BIG BROADCAST OF 1938

Words and Music by LEO ROBIN
and RALPH RAINGER

THERE IS NO GREATER LOVE

Words by MARTY SYMES
Music by ISHAM JONES

THIS CAN'T BE LOVE

from THE BOYS FROM SYRACUSE

Words by LORENZ HART
Music by RICHARD RODGERS

THE VERY THOUGHT OF YOU

Words and Music by
RAY NOBLE

TWO SLEEPY PEOPLE

from the Paramount Motion Picture THANKS FOR THE MEMORY

Words by FRANK LOESSER
Music by HOAGY CARMICHAEL

WHAT'S NEW?

Words by JOHNNY BURKE
Music by BOB HAGGART

Slowly

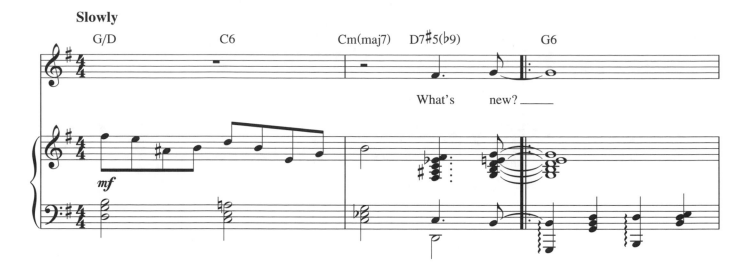

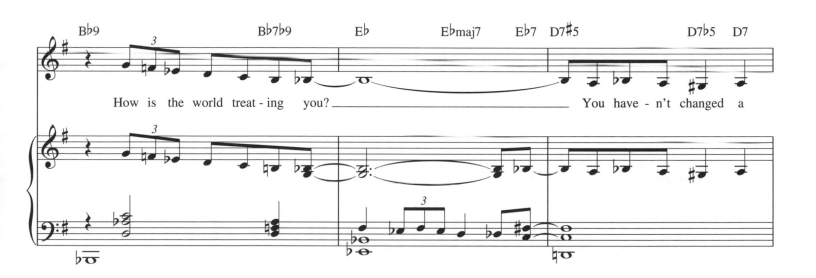

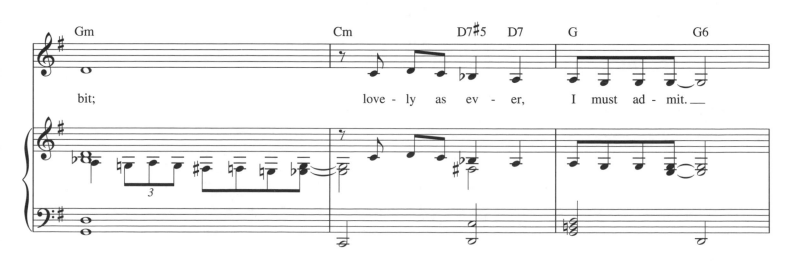

386

WHERE OR WHEN
from BABES IN ARMS

Words by LORENZ HART
Music by RICHARD RODGERS

YESTERDAYS

from ROBERTA
from LOVELY TO LOOK AT

Words by OTTO HARBACH
Music by JEROME KERN

Yes - ter - days, yes - ter - days, days I knew as
youth was mine, truth was mine, joy - ous, free and

hap - py, sweet se - ques - tered days.
flam - ing life, for - sooth, was mine.

YOU BROUGHT A NEW KIND OF LOVE TO ME

from the Paramount Picture THE BIG POND

Words and Music by SAMMY FAIN,
IRVING KAHAL and PIERRE NORMAN

YOU ARE MY SUNSHINE

Words and Music by JIMMIE DAVIS
and CHARLES MITCHELL